FINDING GOD at Yellowstone

A 30 Day Devotional Journey

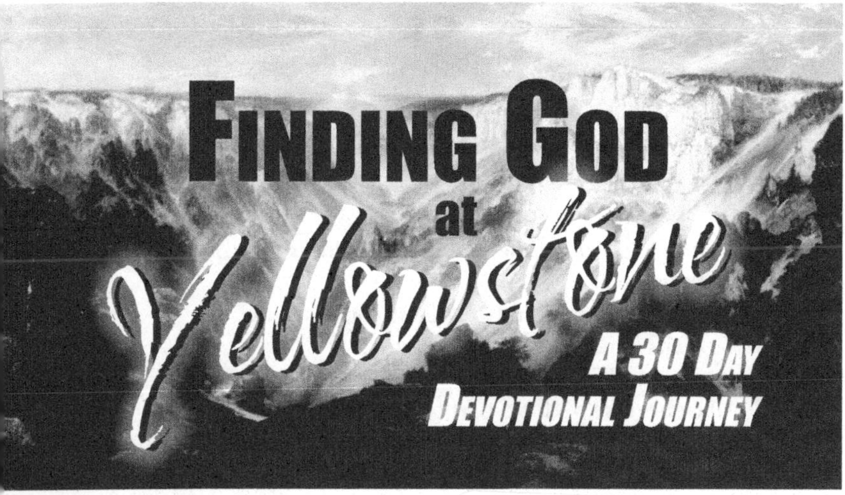

Sammy Thale

Finding God at Yellowstone: 30 Devotions to Inspire Your Faith in God
Daily Devotions from Great Destinations Series

Published by TheBiblePeople.com. Our mission is to encourage people to read, understand, and apply the Bible.

Printed in the United States of America.

Contents

Reading 1
Finding God at Yellowstone: Set Apart

Psalm 118: 20 *"This is the gate of the Lord; the righteous shall enter through it." (NIV)*

On top of the Roosevelt Arch, at the North entrance of Yellowstone, is the inscription, "For the Benefit and Enjoyment of the People". Through the Arch is a rather ordinary scene of mountains and grassland. Perhaps you may feel some disappointment, as if all the talk you have heard about the spectacular beauty of the place is more advertising hype than anything else. It does look so very ordinary.

However, this place was set aside for our benefit and enjoyment. This place called to the hearts of explorers, law-makers, and ordinary people to be set aside. In an age similar to our own, where greed and corruption seemed to reign, this piece of land was set apart for something decidedly different. In 1870, no one would have realized the unique biodiversity of Yellowstone. There was no real recognition that this place had to be conserved for future generations. In that age, as in this, this precious piece of land should have been exploited, and through that exploitation, destroyed. Yet, it was set aside to provide us all with a preserved place where, if we are willing, we can hear the voice of God speak through his marvelous creation.

Perhaps we are a lot like this Roosevelt entrance, rather ordinary and not necessarily meeting our own advertising hype; however, we know that we are set apart. We are set apart to do God's work in all its ordinary magnificence. In Yellowstone, we have the privilege to be set apart to enjoy this very special place, and to hear God speaking through grand attractions and small ordinary encounters. The challenge is whether we will respond to God's invitation. The challenge is also to turn off our cell phones and other technology, and simply be with our

companions and with God. The challenge is to listen rather than to speak, and to enjoy rather than exploit.

Wherever you enter Yellowstone, take a moment to look through the Gate. Take a couple of deep breaths and feel the land call to your heart. You will be able to hear the voice of God gently leading you into this place of rest, renewal, and enjoyment.

Prayer: Holy Father, help me to listen to you in this magnificent place. Holy Jesus, help me to renew my relationship with you through the enjoyment of this place. Holy Spirit, bind me in love to this place, and to the people and creatures with whom I will share it.

Wherever you enter Yellowstone, take a moment to look through the Gate. Take a couple of deep breaths and feel the land call to your heart.

Reading 2
Mammoth Hot Springs: Barren and Beautiful

Psalm 139: 8 *"If I go up to the heavens, you are there; if I make my bed in the depths, you are there." (NIV)*

THROUGH MANY THOUSANDS of years, this barren place had been forming: a slow molding of heat, minerals, and water. It formed under the gaze of God, without human involvement or interference. It was known to God before it was known to us. It has always been beautiful and, despite appearances, it sustains life. Hundreds upon thousands of micro-organisms and bacteria create beautiful shades of oranges, pinks, yellows, greens, and browns.

Look around at the calcium carbonate deposits; some looking like rivers flowing, others looking like terraces. You may have a feeling of desolation. You may be privileged enough to see the mists trailing over the terraces, giving them an eerie quality. It can seem like a place of myths and legends, of spirits and fairies, or a place of extreme nothingness. A place where God refuses to dwell.

Aren't there times when our hearts seem barren, and reflect the starkness of this place? Are there not times when our hearts are filled with myths and legends of our own making, that tell us lies and tales about our Creator? We come to points in our lives when we believe that God cannot, or will not, dwell with us because we cannot sustain the life to which we are called.

However, take time to look again. Look at the careful molding of the rock and minerals. Breathe in the smell of lime. Look at the wonderful colors and textures, and know that God created this place. Know that God created it both barren and beautiful. Know that God is with you in your places of barrenness and that God will make them beautiful. Also know that our barren places do bring forth life if we keep walking with God.

Prayer: Gracious Creator God, help me to trust that you create my barren places, as well as my places of joy. Gentle Christ, help me to realize that my barren places are a mirror of yours, in the desert and in the Garden of Gethsemane. Loving Spirit, keep challenging me to move through my barren places to those of new life and new birth. Holy God, thank you for my barren places, they are as beautiful and as holy as my places of abundance.

Also know that our barren places do bring forth life if we keep walking with God.

Reading 3
Forces of the Northern Range Trail (between Mammoth Hot Springs and Tower Junction): To be Tried by Fire

Acts 2:3-4: *"They saw what seemed to be tongues of fire that separated and came to rest on each of them. All of them were filled with the Holy Spirit." (NIV)*

THIS HALF-MILE BOARDWALK trail was built in 1988, after out-of-control forest fires ravaged Yellowstone and beyond. The fires burned for months and were only put out with the cool temperatures of autumn and the winter snows. However, the vegetation began recovering almost immediately. Fireweed began reappearing within days of the fires being put out. This easy walk is a unique opportunity to learn about the effects of the fires on the environment and to marvel at the recovery of nature.

Fire has always played an important role in both the Jewish and Christian traditions. We find God revealing himself in a burning bush, we have Daniel and his companions being tried by fire, and the disciples were anointed by fire at Pentecost. In the Catholic and Episcopalian tradition, the new fire is lit in the dawn of Easter morning. This new fire then lights the Baptismal candle as the priest proclaims "Christ our Light". Fire is a powerful presence and a central image of our understanding of God.

The Yellowstone fire gives us an imperfect glimpse into this reality. Through the destruction and devastation, from which no one thought the natural wonder of the park would recover, green shoots and leaves began to appear almost immediately. Over 9,000 fire fighters and 4,000 military personnel risked their lives for this beautiful space. This human sacrifice is nothing less than astounding. As destructive as this fire was, it could not overwhelm the power of our Creator God. It did not overwhelm our ability to work with God to protect and preserve creation. Take in this space as you savor new life and witness recovery. From the restoration of the scrub lands to the eventual flourishing of the forest, God is constantly at work. God is never overwhelmed and never consumed.

Prayer: Creator God, anoint me with the fire of your Holy Spirit to live out my calling to serve you. Help me never to be overwhelmed by destruction, but always look for signs of new life, because they are always there.

From the restoration of
the scrub lands to the eventual
flourishing of the forest, God is
constantly at work.

Reading 4
Yellowstone National Park: Fasting to Feast

Luke 13: 34 "*...how often I have longed to gather your children together, as a hen gathers her chicks under her wings...*" *(NIV)*

YOU WILL SPEND a lot of time in Yellowstone travelling from one place to another. In our technological age, there may be music playing, the kids may be watching DVDs in the back of the car, and there may be constant communication via cell phone to family, friends, and even the office. These are not bad things in and of themselves, but they do clutter the mind and crowd out the nurturing tenor of God's voice. Thus, the challenge is to declare a fast from these things for a portion of your driving. It can be the first ten minutes at the start of the day, or you can fast for longer stretches. Allow the beauty of this place to nurture you. Feast your eyes on the mountains, the forests, the streams, and rivers. Watch how the light plays with the landscape, and how the colors of the park change as the sun moves during the day. Let God's creation nurture you.

If you are travelling with kids, discuss what they are seeing. Talk about colors, light, and texture—this is a way of helping them feast and be nurtured by nature, to be nurtured by God.

Also take this time to drive a little more slowly. Take time to lift your eyes to the magnificent Rocky Mountains and be nurtured by God. Why is this important? Most of our lives are frantic, and our spiritual lives mirror this frenzy. We wake up in the morning, read our devotions or say our morning prayers, and perhaps try and set aside some contemplative time, but our minds are spinning around all the things that need to be done. Then we rush into the day; work, school, and church activities. We collapse into bed with an overwhelmed "Thank you, Lord", only to begin again early in the morning. Once again, these things are not bad in and of themselves and life is, for the most part, fulfilling. However, the magnificence of the Rockies reminds us that we need to slow down and really look. God is not asking us to get anywhere or achieve anything. God is being incredibly extravagant and is asking you to rest in this and feast on this. Allow God to nurture you.

Think of this fast as climbing, as small children do with their parents, into the lap of God for a wonderful cuddle. Some of us will do this for a couple of minutes, and others will fall asleep here. It does not matter. Simply take some time to do this, take time to be in the lap of God, and allow God to nurture you.

Prayer: Help me to rest in the magnificence, the extravagance of what God has created. Help me to create the time to be nurtured. Help me to feast on the Rockies and know that they reflect the extravagant love that You have for me.

The magnificence of the Rockies reminds us that we need to slow down and really look.

Reading 5
On coming upon the Grand Canyon of Yellowstone for the first time: Fall on your knees

Revelation 4:11 "*You are worthy, our Lord and God, to receive glory and honor and power, for you created all things, and by your will they were created and have their being.*" *(NIV)*

THE MAJOR CATACLYSMIC forces that combined to mold this place are not well understood; however, what is known is that it was an eclectic combination of volcanic eruptions, seismic shifts, glaciers, and the normal wear and tear of wind and rain. Geologists, palaeontologists, and other scientists have spent their careers studying this place. Many could describe to you, in detail, what you are seeing. However, when you first come upon this place of indescribable, overwhelming grandeur, is your first response scientific? In the pause between seeing this magnificence and translating what you are seeing into words, what is your response? This canyon, through its very existence, gives God glory and honor and praise. It shouts out the power of its Creator, so loudly that we should be stunned into an awed silence, and we should shout out, "We believe!".

This canyon echoes with the voices of angels crying, "Holy, holy, holy, God of power and might, heaven and earth are full of your glory, Hosanna in the highest!". Is our response to join the chorus? It is filled with the voice of the God of Moses saying, "I am who I am" (Exodus 3:14). Is our response to tremble and fall on our knees? It is the voice of the prophets thundering through the ages, "Prepare the way of the Lord!" (Mark 1:2-3). Are we ready for this

challenge? It is the voice of Jesus saying, "Who do you say that I am?" (Mark 8:29). Can we answer, "You are the Christ, the son of God!"? In the space between seeing and naming, between one breath and another, where thought is not thought but feeling, how do we respond?

Prayer: "Holy, holy, holy, God of power and might, heaven and earth are full of your Glory, Hosanna in the Highest. Blessed is He who comes in the Name of the Lord, Hosanna in the highest!"

This canyon, through its very existence, gives God glory and honor and praise.

Reading 6
Inspiration Point— Looking down the Canyon: The Angels cry Holy

Revelation 11:17 "*We give thanks to you, Lord God Almighty, the One who is and who was, because you have taken your great power and have begun to reign". (NIV)*

LIFE BATTERS AND bruises us all. We make bad choices, good people have horrible things happen to them, and the world seems to be filled with corruption and lies. Many of us face crushing financial woes, some of us bear wounds in our hearts that defy our attempts at healing, and some of us have had to cope with the death of those we love. The litany of our deep pain and suffering goes on. In that litany, we can lose the voices of the angels that declare through eternity that God has taken up his great power and begun to reign. We hear the voices that ask, "Where is your God now?" This canyon is your answer, "God is here".

In recognizing the presence of the power God, we are not negating that our suffering is real. We are affirming that God's power is greater than our suffering. We are not denying that we will continue to feel pain, worry, and anxiety. We are affirming that God is present in these moments. As the angels proclaim the power of God, as their cries and songs rebound across the walls of the canyon, hear God's voice offering you a place to lay down your burdens, because God has taken up great power and begun to reign. Throw your sorrows and burdens into this massive expression of God's power and, if even for a small moment, experience the relief of your suffering. For many of us, this will be brief and momentary, but it is a small taste of God's power over death. It is a promise of resurrection. Hold onto this promise as you leave this place. For a moment, cry out with the angels: "Holy, holy, holy!". Trust that God does reign in both this world and in the one to come.

Prayer: Holy, holy, holy, Lord God Almighty, all your works praise your Name. Lift my burdens for a moment so that I can hear the angel voices, lift the scales from my eyes so that I can experience your great power. Help me to cherish this moment when I can know that you reign.

Trust that God does reign in both this world and in the one to come.

Reading 7
Inspiration Point— Looking up the Canyon: "Who do you say that I am?"

Matthew 16:16 *"Simon Peter answered, 'You are the Christ, the Son of the living God.' " (NIV)*

IN THE EXTRAVAGANCE of the wonder of the Yellowstone Grand Canyon, we can get caught up in the voices of the angels and neglect the still small voice that asks, "Who do you say that I am?" This was the question that Jesus asked of Peter, and asks of each one of us. As we glory in the creative power of God, we can forget that in acknowledging God as Creator we also have to acknowledge God as Redeemer. We have to answer Jesus' question to us, "Who do you say that I am?"

Take a couple of moments to gaze up this canyon and let this question settle in your heart. There have been pages and pages of scholarly (and not so scholarly) writing on the "correct" answer to this question. Thousands have spilt their blood for the right to impose answers to this question on others. We can point to our traditions, creeds, and doctrines for intellectual answers to this question. However, Jesus is asking you, "Who do you say that I am?" In this place, you don't really need to provide an answer to it, you simply have to hear it. Hopefully, in hearing the question in this place that shouts the reality of the existence of God, we can train ourselves to hear this question in other places where God appears to be absent. Can we hear the question when we are angry with spouses and children, when we lose our jobs, or when human dignity is ignored? Can we hear this question each time we are confronted with our own fallibility and humanity, and the fallibility of others? And, in these situations, can we answer like Peter, "You are the Christ, the son of God," and act accordingly?

Prayer: Holy Jesus, help me to ponder the question, "Who do you say that I am?". Help me to hear this question as I live out my calling. Help me to answer the question through the service of my life.

Jesus is asking you, "Who do you say that I am?"

Reading 8
Yellowstone Grand Canyon—Lower Falls: Hidden Promises

Genesis 9:13 *"And God said, 'This is the sign of the covenant I am making between me and you and every living creature with you, a covenant for all generations to come.'"* (NIV)

AT CERTAIN TIMES of the year, at certain times of the day, a rainbow appears at Lower Falls. You can plan to be either at Lookout or Artist's Point to see it, but most of us will see these beautiful falls without the addition of the rainbow. Just because we don't see it does not mean it does not exist. In the Ancient Hebrew scriptures, we find the story of Noah and the flood. Most of us have heard the story again and again; and thus, its power and impact have been lost to many of us. It is not the cute story of school plays or children's songs with catchy lyrics. It is the story of the first covenant that God makes with humanity.

In the drama of the covenant of Abraham and Moses, and the pathos of the covenant God makes through Christ, this very first covenant is often forgotten. Here, God promises never to destroy the earth through flood again. This promise is reflected through the gentleness and beauty of a rainbow. Therefore, in the roar of the waters of Lower Falls, remember that God makes promises. In this first covenant there are also several implied promises that are true for us today. God promises to care for the earth, God promises that He wants a relationship with us, and God promises never to destroy us. These promises come to fulfilment through our relationship with Christ. Each time a rainbow appears, remember God's promises. In the roar of the waters, remember God's promises, and in the stillness of your heart know that God continues to make these promises to you each and every day.

Prayer: I find peace in the roar of your waters. I remember you as I close my eyes in sleep and wake to greet the morning. Your promises of care and love are eternal. Help me to remember and remind me with rainbows when I forget.

In the roar of the waters,
remember God's promises, and
in the stillness of your heart know
that God continues to make these
promises to you each and
every day.

Reading 9
The Artist's Paint Pots: Mud, Mud, Glorious Mud

Genesis 1:31 "*God saw all that he had made, and it was very good.*" *(NIV)*

Boiling mud. Mud so hot that it will scald you if you touch it. It seems a bit frivolous, a bit useless. However, from a God who created seahorses, hammer-head sharks, and wildebeest, it does not seem so strange.

Human beings tend to take the business of living a bit too seriously. Everything has a purpose and a use. We tell ourselves that we also have a purpose and a use. We need to be good parents, excel in our chosen career, and be "the best" in whatever we do. Doing all of puts huge pressure on us to "succeed" and we can end up taking very little time to enjoy life's little idiosyncrasies—like boiling mud. We can take very little time to relax, to laugh, and to simply enjoy our friendship with God.

God has made the strangest, most beautiful things, and you will see them all over Yellowstone. Take some time to look for them. From the elk, to amazing crawling insects, to natural wonders, enjoy God's sense of humor. Hear the mud baths go, "plop, plop, plop," and perhaps hear our Creator laugh along with you. Look at your little toe. It has no use or purpose but it looks so amazing on a newborn's little foot. Look at snowflakes. Not every single snowflake needs to be different but they are, perhaps, just for the fun of it. God's laughter and creative joy is heard far and wide throughout creation, so let us hear it and let us share it.

Prayer: Creator God, thank you for all the strange wonders of this place. Help me to laugh with you and enjoy what you have created. Help me find the little things within your creation that make me laugh. Help me to share this laughter with you.

Not every single snowflake needs to be different but they are, perhaps, just for the fun of it

Reading 10
Yellowstone Grand Canyon—Point Sublime:Places of Peace

Isaiah 55:12 *"You will go out in joy and be led forth in peace; the mountains and hills will burst into song before you, and all the trees of the field will clap their hands."* (NIV)

THIS IS DEFINITELY a place to stop and take a deep breath. This point has been described as "pretty, beautiful, picturesque, magnificent, grand, sublime, awful, and terrible". Awful, as in full of awe? According to the dictionary, besides being synonymous with terrible, awful also means "with great reverence". This is a meaning of awful that we may have forgotten. So let us, at this place, choose to approach God's creation with great reverence.

Think of Yellowstone as a great cathedral created by God. No human stone mason could carve out the rock with as much skill and beauty as God has done. No artist could have covered the walls with such beautiful colors. During the different seasons, you will see an ever-changing display of greens and browns, yellows and golds, blues and whites. As

you look at this place, see the mountains rising up in reverence to our Creator God. There is a sense of hushed awe.

Let this awe fill your heart and mind. Say with the father of the boy freed from an unclean spirit, "I believe, help my unbelief"(Mark 9:24). Let this place bring you to a point of silence and reflection. Let this cathedral bring you to a point of such reverence that your mind is quiet and you can rest in the peace of God.

Prayer: Holy God, the creator of all things, your creation leaves me full of awe. In the silence of your creation, hear my heart calling to you in reverence. Help me to search for you in the beauty of this place.

Let this awe fill your heart and mind.

Reading 11
Yellowstone Norris Geyser Basin—Porcelain Basin: Explosions

Psalms 121:1-2 *"I lift up my eyes to the hills—where does my help come from? My help comes from the Lord, the Maker of heaven and earth." (NIV)*

COLORS, HISSING STEAM, and sulphuric odors all combine to make the Norris Geyser Basin one of the most popular attractions in Yellowstone. It is also one of the most beautiful. Standing and looking at the Porcelain Basin, you see beautiful hydrothermal pools and explosions. These are so dramatic that they may prevent you from looking further. Lift your eyes and see the forest of pine trees that ring the Basin, and then look even further and see the majestic Rockies rising in the distance.

The Psalmist reminds us to look up to the mountains. It is a reminder that we can spend a great deal of time caught up in the beauty of creation without recognizing the Creator. In this particular space, we can spend hours looking at the drama of the hydrothermal pools, and we forget that there is more. We can forget that within creation we are meeting with the Creator. Take some time to look up. Remember that you are searching for the God who made all this beauty. You are also trusting that, as you are searching, you will find him and he will bring you help.

Prayer: I lift my eyes to the hills from where comes my help. It comes from you, Creator God. It comes from you, Jesus Christ. You do not slumber and you do not sleep, you send your angels to surround me with your love and protection. Holy Spirit, help me to always search within creation for the One God; Father, Son, and Holy Spirit.

We can forget that within creation
we are meeting with the Creator.

Reading 12
Yellowstone Norris Geyser Basin—Black Growler Steam Vent: The fires of Hell cannot consume us

Matthew 6:33 *"But seek first his kingdom and his righteousness." (NIV)*

THE BLACK GROWLER Steam Vent has measured temperatures from 199 up to 280 degrees F, thus one could quite possibly say that it is a steam vent into Hell. Hell gets quite a lot of airtime in some Christian quarters. We have the current (and not so current) slew of movies about vampires, demons, and other members of Satan's army. In some classic literature, the character of Satan is far more appealing than the character of any of the good angels. One of the stage directions reads, "and Satan appears with fire coming out of every bodily opening" - this boggles the imagination and must have been quite a spectacular sight. We seem to be fascinated by the nature of true evil, and some people even try to seek it out.

Firstly, we need to remember that we must always seek the kingdom of God. No matter how attractive evil is, we are reminded that we need to "flee evil and cling to what is good". Secondly, when we stumble onto evil, as is inevitable, we need to remember that the "gates of hell" cannot prevail against God. Thus, if we believe and trust in God, there is no place we can go, no battle into which we will enter, and no demon that we will face, that is stronger than the God who surrounds us. Let this hot Yellowstone geyser remind you of this. It is not our calling to seek out evil, it is our responsibility to believe and trust that Christ has power over all things and that we are surrounded by God's love and protection.

Prayer: Help me to seek your Kingdom. Help me to trust in yourencompassing love and protection. Help me to know that when I do struggle with evil, when I am confronted with something that appears to overwhelm me, you are there surrounding me with your loving protection.

The Black Growler Steam Vent has measured temperatures from 199 up to 280 degrees F, thus one could quite possibly say that it is a steam vent into Hell.

Reading 13
Yellowstone Norris Geyser Basin—Steamboat Geyser: Consistency

Hebrews 13: *"Jesus Christ is the same yesterday and today and forever"*. *(NIV)*

THE STEAMBOAT GEYSER is the world's tallest active geyser. The eruptions of this geyser are completely unpredictable. You may see a magnificent show, or you may see very little. The latter is the most likely. God is not inconsistent like this geyser. God is always loving, always calling us into relationship. It is God who reached out to us in the person of Jesus. It is the Holy Spirit who sustains our life. However, we often want God to be consistent on our own terms. We want God to pour blessings on us, but not onto our neighbors because they are "sinners". We want God to punish someone else's sins but forgive our own.

Making God in our own image is a very dangerous business, because it makes God human, and God is not a fallible human being. The consistency we find in God is that God is love. This is the essence of God's very being, and therefore it should be the essence of ours. By following the path of love that God shows us, we begin to love ourselves and others, and we deepen our love for God. By following the way of the cross, we learn the comfort of having the friendship and support of Jesus. By allowing the Holy Spirit to breathe love into us, we become more able to reflect the love of God. We become more constant in faith, hope, and love. Thus, we may not see Steamboat Geyser blowing its mighty top, but we can trust that we will definitely see the face of God.

Prayer: Let me always seek your face. Let me always see you in others. Let me follow in your footsteps of love.

The Steamboat Geyser is the world's tallest active geyser. The eruptions of this geyser are completely unpredictable. You may see a magnificent show, or you may see very little.

Reading 14
Yellowstone Norris Geyser Basin—Congress Pool: We are in the world, not of it

Romans 12:2 *"Do not conform any longer to the pattern of this world, but be transformed by the renewing of your mind. Then you will be able to test and approve what God's will is—his good, pleasing and perfect will."* (NIV)

YOU WILL BE seeing a number of these beautiful pools as you walk through the Norris Geyser Basin. Beautiful and serene, the minerals of the pools absorb all the colors of the spectrum except for blue, which is reflected back to us in the color of this pool. Blue is a cool color, even when forming part of a hot spring. It is ethereal and otherworldly. In Eastern iconography, Mary, the mother of Jesus, is almost always pictured with a blue cloak draped around her, to signify that her response to God was beautiful and somehow otherworldly.

As you walk through and look at these pools, remember that through Christ you are also part of a different kingdom. It is one in which God reigns over all, where sorrowing and sighing are no more. It is this world that we strive to reflect into our own. In our response to God, do we bring God's kingdom into this world as Mary did? Do we speak words of comfort and joy to those who suffer? Do we live our lives with integrity? Do we reflect the wisdom, love, and compassion of Christ to every one we meet?

Let these pools remind you that you are, first and foremost, part of the kingdom of God. Take comfort from this. However, your responsibility is to reflect this kingdom back into the world through your words and actions.

Prayer: Lord, I thank you that I am part of a kingdom in which you reign. Thank you for giving me the opportunity to reflect this into a world where your love and compassion seem absent. Help me take comfort and strength from living in your kingdom and loving in the world.

Let these pools remind you that you are, first and foremost, part of the kingdom of God.

Reading 15
Yellowstone Norris Geyser Basin—Minute Geyser Basin: Decisions, Decisions

Ephesians 5:9 *"For this light within you produces only what is good and right and true." (NLT)*

MINUTE GEYSER WAS once one of the main attractions of Yellowstone. It erupted 40-70 feet every minute. However, early visitors to the park threw stones and rocks into the geyser, possibly trying to see how far the geyser would spit these out, or how heavy a rock needed to be before the great force of the geyser could not lift the weight. Over the years, the geyser became clogged until it became the small, irregular geyser you see today.

Human beings are a thoughtless species. We can do things without thinking of the consequences, and this small, insignificant little geyser reminds us of that. In contrast, Jesus always knew the consequences of his actions even as they led him into conflict with authority. However, his actions also led him into deep

and special friendships with his disciples. By thinking through our actions, both for good and for ill, we may be surprised by the direction that life takes. The people who set this park aside had the foresight and wisdom to know that this place would need protection. They were thinking about the consequences of their actions. Those people who threw rocks into the geyser gave no thought to tomorrow and what their actions would mean. The question is, will our lives reflect the glory of Yellowstone or the insipidity of Minute Geyser? Will we make decisions thinking with "the mind of Christ", or will we simply throw rocks in all directions and wait to see what happens?

Prayer: Holy Jesus, help me to see the world through your eyes and to make decisions using your mind. Thank you for the reminders all around us that thoughtful decisions do have beautiful consequences.

Those people who threw rocks into the geyser gave no thought to tomorrow and what their actions would mean.

Reading 16
Old Faithful Geyser:Finding God

1 Corinthians 13:12 *"For now we see through a glass, darkly; but then face to face: now I know in part; but then shall I know even as also I am known." (KJV)*

OLD FAITHFUL IS the most predictable of Yellowstone's Geysers and almost all visitors will time their journeys so that they can see an eruption. The Geyser starts by "playing," with small eruptions that get larger and larger until they reach a height of at least 90 feet. It is certainly a spectacular sight that will keep you enraptured. It is almost like the Geyser is playing with us, drawing us into a state of anticipation and excitement until it delivers the big dramatic finish. Does this not reflect how God sometimes draws us deeper into relationship?

We know that when we die, we will meet our beloved Lord. This will be the point at which we will finally see Christ face-to-face. However, until then, we see through the glass darkly. We see God breaking through into our lives and into the lives of those whom we love. We notice that we have grown

deeper in expressing faith, hope, and love. We may feel barren and spiritually dry, but we trust that God is leading us on. We hold onto the anticipation of meeting our beloved. This Geyser at play mirrors that wondrous anticipation as we are drawn into the life of God. We know that there will be an explosion of joy when we finally see our Maker, Redeemer and Friend. However, for the moment we need to enjoy the journey and watch in amazement as Old Faithful explodes, reflecting God's continued joy in the life that He has created.

Prayer: I only see you "darkly" now, but I will grow into seeing you face-to-face. Help me to enjoy the journey, help me to trust that the journey will lead me to you, and help me to grow in faith, hope and love.

Watch in amazement as Old Faithful explodes, reflecting God's continued joy in the life that He has created.

Reading 17 Yellowstone Geyser Basin—Doublet Pools:Cries of Deliverance

Psalms 46:1-2 *"God is our refug and strength, an ever-present help in trouble. Therefore we will not fear, though the earth give way and the mountains fall into the heart of the sea." (NIV)*

THE DOUBLET POOLS are a particularly beautiful geological feature and a favorite spot for photographers. Although geysers have been known to erupt at this pool, these are very infrequent. The most that you will experience is a minor shaking of the ground. It is believed that collapsing steam bubbles deep underground cause these tremors.

Sometimes we experience "minor shaking of the ground". We wake up one morning, unsure of whether God exists. We go about our daily lives and realize we haven't thought about God in weeks. We continue our regular church involvement and suddenly realize that we have not heard a sermon properly, or genuinely participated in worship for months. Our ground shakes. Perhaps we question whether we are genuine Christians as we struggle and strive to feel God's presence and to know God's will.

When we experience these doubts and fears, they are minor tremblings of our faith. Just like the trembling that you may experience here, they are a normal part of being in relationship with God. The earth is not moved, there are no grand explosions, and you are not going to leave your faith behind. However, as you experience these small times of crisis, know that God is there with you. Even if the earth does give way, God will be with you. God will surround your soul

with cries of deliverance (Psalms 32:7).

Prayer: Holy God, I thank you that your creation reminds us that you are always with us. Holy Jesus, thank you for being our friend even through our doubt. Holy Spirit, please surround my soul with cries of love, and cries of deliverance.

God is there with you. Even if the earth does give way, God will be with you.

Reading 18
Yellowstone Geyser Basin—Old Faithful Observation Point: Be Still and Know

Psalms 46:10 *"Be still, and know that I am God." (NIV)*

Take a couple of minutes to look out onto this beautiful panorama. Drink in Old Faithful erupting, look at the views that you have of the other geysers, and take some time to appreciate where you are. If you were the only person on earth, this place would still exist and you would be able to drink it in, as you are doing now. It was made for God's pleasure and was set apart for your enjoyment.

In the rush for some of us to "see everything", to take pictures of every magnificent sight, to tick items off our "to do" list, we can miss the absolute awesomeness of what we are seeing. At this point, whether you are at the beginning or end of your stay, take some time to be silent with God. Enjoy what has been created.

Remember that you have also been created. That you were created for God's pleasure and set apart for His enjoyment. You are even more wild and more wonderful than the scene you see before you, and God takes great delight in spending this time with you. Imagine that Jesus is standing next to you, perhaps with his hand in yours, also looking at this marvelous scene. He is sharing all your emotions and feelings. As the wind blows, even if it brings sulphurous-smelling air into your nostrils, remember that the Holy Spirit is even closer to you than this air which you are breathing. Hear the whole of creation whispering and shouting, "God loves you!". Rest in this message. You will walk away from this scene, but God will not walk away from you. Carry this in your heart as you remain still for a while, holding onto the hand of Christ, your brother and friend.

Prayer: You are in the midst of us and I am called by your name. You will not forsake me, O Lord, my God.

You will walk away from this scene, but God will not walk away from you.

Reading 19

Yellowstone Geyser Basin—Beauty Pool: Hidden Workings

1 Corinthians 4:5 "*Therefore judge nothing before the appointed time; wait till the Lord comes. He will bring to light what is hidden in darkness and will expose the motives of men's hearts." (NIV)*

THE BEAUTY POOL is another truly indescribable sight within this Yellowstone Geyser Basin. The pool seems to go on forever into the depths of the earth. For many, if not most, of the geothermal wonders that you are seeing, scientists do not know what causes them. For example, Beauty Pool is closely related to Chromatic Spring; as the level of one rises, the level of the other falls. However, we do not know why this cycle sometimes repeats itself within monthly intervals and sometimes within yearly intervals.

In our eyes, there are many things that are hidden, especially in the depths of our hearts. Sometimes we do not even understand these ourselves. There are hidden hurts that ensure that we hurt others when we feel threatened. There are misunderstandings that shape our attitudes and beliefs. There are also joys that we have experienced in childhood that we want our loved ones to experience. There are hidden talents that we may, one day, contribute to the world. Our hearts are as deep, beautiful, and as unfathomable as this amazing pool. God sees all of this. Just like God knows the hidden workings of these pools, God knows the hidden workings of our hearts.

This has two implications. The first is, and it is the one on which we often focus, God knows our sins. Scripture is very clear that these sins will be exposed before the gaze of God and we will be judged. What we often forget is that it is our whole heart which will be exposed. This leads us to the fact that all that is good,

true, and beautiful will also be held within God's gaze. By only thinking of hidden things within our hearts as sinful, we can lose out on a deeper relationship with God. This pool, in all its beauty, can help to remind us that our hidden heart contains both beauty and ugliness. That which is hidden in our hearts is our relationship with our Creator, Redeemer, and Friend. This is a complex and beautiful relationship. Marred by sin, absolutely, but also shot through by light and love.

Prayer: Holy God, help me to see that the beauty of nature is reflected in the beauty of my heart. Help me to trust that even though I may feel crushed by the damaging effects of sin, you see my whole heart. You also see that it is beautiful. Holy Spirit, help me always to know that at every moment of every day, the hidden depths of my heart are open to you. Holy Jesus, help me to know that through your resurrection my heart is filled with your saving love.

This pool, in all its beauty, can help to remind us that our hidden heart contains both beauty and ugliness.

Reading 20
Yellowstone Geyser Basin—Morning Glory Pool:A Crust around your Soul

Romans 8:27 *"And he who searches our hearts knows the mind of the Spirit, because the Spirit intercedes for the saints in accordance with God's will." (NIV)*

THE MORNING GLORY Pool is considered one of the most beautiful features to be seen in the Geyser Basin. However, even though it looks spectacular with its large rim of orange and yellow bacteria, this is not its "natural" state. Over the years, visitors have thrown coins, rubble, and other debris into the pool. This has had the effect of a temperature drop that has produced what you see today. The bacteria have become like a crust around the beautiful blue calm of the pool.

This is similar to the effect that sin has on us, both those we have committed and those sins that others have committed. We have experienced how others have hurt us. We have all experienced betrayal at very deep levels. We have been disappointed and angered by others. We have done things that we never would have imagined, as we have tried to deal with our own hurt and fear. In effect, we have thrown rubble into the beautiful space we call "the soul". It has been wounded, and we have developed a crust that has changed the perfection in which we were created.

Although the soul does remain beautiful, these woundings do change it,uch like human vandalism has changed the Morning Glory Pool. However, unlike this pool, even with deep sin, we can begin to conform to the mind of Christ. We can confess our sins, our hurt, and our pain to God. This is the unconditional promise that Jesus makes to us: I intercede on your behalf (Romans 8:34). We are battered and bruised, and we batter and bruise, but the Holy Spirit will forever urge us, compel us even, to continually confess our sins and to forgive those of others. It is through this confession that the crust of hurt and fear begins to diminish and we can better see the beauty of the soul to which we are called.

Prayer: Lord Jesus Christ, Son of God, have mercy on me, a sinner. Lord Jesus Christ, Son of God, have mercy on me, a sinner. Lord Jesus Christ, Son of God, have mercy on me, a sinner.

It is through this confession that the crust of hurt and fear begins to diminish and we can better see the beauty of the soul to which we are called.

Reading 21
Fountainpaint—Celestine Pools: Your Hands

John 5:7 " *'Sir', the invalid replied, 'I have no one to help me into the pool when the water is stirred. While I am trying to get in, someone else goes down ahead of me.'* " *(NIV)*

On first coming across this pool, one sighs automatically at its beauty. Deep, calm and serene, it seems to have existed for eternity. Perhaps this is a reflection of the pool that the angel stirred so that people who were blind, lame, and paralyzed could enter and be healed.

The invalid whom Jesus encountered at the pool had waited 38 years for healing, and no one had helped him towards this healing. It is a cliché to say that "Jesus has no hands but ours", but the problem with clichés is that they are often true. The challenge that comes through to us from the story of the pool is one that Jesus poses to his disciples: "who is going to help bring the blind, the lame, and the paralyzed to me?" Thinking back on your own Christian journey: who helped you to come to Christ, who helped you in your times of need, who sang with you in your times of joy? Each one of these people, whether known or unknown, helped you towards a relationship with Christ and into the healing pool of his love. How have you passed this gift on? How have you walked with the people who God gave you to love in their times of joy and sorrow? Have you been able to show, by your friendship and care, a path to Jesus?

Prayer: Thank you for all the hands and hearts that have led me to you. Thank you for the privilege of being able to help others into the healing waters of your love. Help me to continue to be your hands in this world.

How have you walked with the people who God gave you to love in their times of joy and sorrow? Have you been able to show, by your friendship and care, a path to Jesus?

Reading 22

Yellowstone Lake: The Dawn

Psalms 57:8 *"Awake, my soul! Awake, harp and lyre! I will awaken the dawn."* (NIV)

MOST OF US will still be sleeping when the dawn light begins to awaken Yellowstone. We will not see the sun gently rising on Yellowstone Lake, we will not see the night, fading into shades of blue, and eventually into the full colors of the morning. For many days, especially in the dead of winter, no human heart will rise with the sun to see this beautiful sight. However, all creation does sing as the sun rises. And it really does not matter when we rise, we can always choose to join this grand song of praise.

Many of us have a morning or evening devotion, where we set aside some time for God. We may use a devotional book or the Divine Office, or any number of aids to prayer. Perhaps, especially while you are at Yellowstone Lake, leave these behind and use the lake as your aid to prayer. Find a place where you can see the beauty of the lake and be still. Allow the song of creation to wash over you. Let your own soul rise up to meet this song. Allow it to lead your soul where it needs to go. It may be a song of joy and thanksgiving, it may be a lamentation of deep pain, or a song of uncertainty. You need to sing these to God because God wants to hear them.

Wake your dawn, whether at 5 am or 10 am, with your harp and lyre, with the genuine song of your heart. It will be heard and the peace of the lake will wash over you, if just for a moment, with God's song of love for you.

Prayer: I will awake the dawn, I will cry out to you with both praise and supplication. You are my Lord and my God and I will thank you.

While you are at Yellowstone Lake, leave these behind and use the lake as your aid to prayer.

Reading 23
Yellowstone Lake: Mount Washburn

Deuteronomy 30:19 *"This day I call heaven and earth as witnesses against you that I have set before you life and death, blessings and curses. Now choose life, so that you and your children may live." (NIV)*

IF YOU ARE going to visit any of the mountains in Yellowstone, this one is the most accessible. Even if you don't take the hike up to the top, the views from the parking way-station are still spectacular. Drink them in. On a clear day, they will seem to go on forever, conveying a sense of freedom and space. This is a gift from God, a reminder that one of the graces we are given is the freedom to choose. Like Joshua, you can choose life or you can choose death. You can choose to walk in the light of Christ or you can choose the dim shadows.

The problem with the dim shadows is that they may feel very safe. If you are at Mount Washburn and mist, rain, or snow surround the mountain, the view will be obscured. You will not be hiking to the top and will probably not move too far away from your car. You will stay put because moving forward seems to be too scary, as it is treacherous. This action is wise on a mountain, but is not wise with God. Choosing to walk in the light compels us forward, enables us to change and grow. Even if the light is so overwhelming that the path ahead is obscured, we can trust that Christ is with us and leading us on. If we choose to stay in the shadows we will never be able to live the full life to which we are all called. Will we choose the freedom that Christ offers or will we choose to stagnate? Will we continue to carry the burdens of

the darkness, especially fear, or will we commit to working towards letting these go as we journey with and into the light?

Freedom of choice is a great blessing and a great responsibility, so choose wisely.

Prayer: Loving Jesus, help me, however gradually, to release my burdens, take your hand, and walk in the light. Holy Spirit, help me to choose life, in all its fullness, every day. Gracious Father, be with me as I make the responsible choices for freedom.

We can trust that Christ is with us and leading us on.

Reading 24

Yellowstone Lake: Two Ocean Plateau

Isaiah 64:1 *"Oh, that you would rend the heavens and come down, that the mountains would tremble before you!" (NIV)*

"O Come, O Come, Emmanuel" is the first line of a well-known Christian hymn. It expresses the longing of God's people for the coming Messiah. It expresses the longing of the world to have their Creator walk on Earth so that sorrowing and sighing will be no more. It is a phrase that is always on our hearts as we wait in the joyful hope of the coming of Christ.

Hopefully, you feel the longing of all creation. The longing deep in your own being to be more and more part of the life of God. Whether you are a "newborn" Christian or one who has been a friend of God for years, this longing is always present, never dissipates, and tends to grow stronger with time. During Christ's life on earth, we hear of his deep longing for his Father, especially through his passion and death. Our longing is an echo of His.

Looking at this lake, we can find some peace in our waiting and longing for God. Only God knows the time and the place when our cry of "Oh Come, Oh Come, Emmanuel" will be answered. This lake will follow its seasons, as it has done for thousands of years, just as we must follow ours. Yet, even as we wait, God is with us. Our cry is answered even as our longing deepens. We find peace, even in times of great turmoil, and we find God when we cry "Oh Come".

Prayer: Oh Come, Oh Come, Emmanuel, redeem your captive. Oh Come, Oh Come, Emmanuel, help me to grow ever deeper. Oh Come, Oh Come, Emmanuel, let me recognize your presence in every season of my life.

Looking at this lake, we can find some peace in our waiting and longing for God.

Reading 25
Yellowstone Lake: Isa Lake

Psalms 118:22 *"The stone the builders rejected has become the capstone." (NIV)*

LAKE ISA SITS on the continental divide, draining both into the Pacific and the Atlantic oceans. Compared to some of the other, more extravagant, sites in Yellowstone, Lake Isa can be a bit of a disappointment. Beautiful, yes, but nothing special. Yet, this is the beginning of the nation's great rivers: the Snake, the Columbia, the Missouri, and the Mississippi.

How often do we underestimate ourselves and others, simply by looking at appearances. A little old lady serving tea at church may also serve tea at a local women's shelter. The young man, full of piercing and tattoos, may be an incredible scientist. The local pastor may be struggling with loneliness so deep that he is drowning this in drink. We never know what is lying just beneath the surface.

We also do not know what lies beneath our own surface of insecurity. We often compare ourselves to great men and women, and we do not look at the greatness within ourselves. Underneath, we may be exceptional parents, wonderful siblings, and loving children, and we all have many gifts and talents to offer the world. Lake Isa, quite and calm and unassuming, reminds us that what appears on the surface does not predict the gifts that can be offered. Look further than the limitations you place upon yourself. Look further than the judgements you make on other people. The gifts that can be revealed may change your world. Furthermore, it is these gifts that God calls us to offer to the building of his kingdom.

Prayer: Holy God, help me to see that everything you have created is good. Help me to see Christ in everyone, including myself. Help me to look for the hidden gifts and talents that we all can offer to the building of your kingdom.

How often do we underestimate ourselves and others, simply by looking at appearances.

Reading 26
Factory Hill: Places of Prayer

Luke 5:16 *"But Jesus often withdrew to lonely places and prayed." (NIV)*

THESE MOUNTAINS WERE named "Factory Hill" by the early explorers, as there were about 50 small geysers around the mountain, which made it look like a big industrial factory. These geysers are inactive now. The beautiful Mount Sheridan can be seen in the background. It seems to invite you to hike on its slopes and explore all its nooks and crannies.

Perhaps it was this invitation that the boy Jesus felt when he went into the hills and mountains of his home. Perhaps it was this invitation that blossomed into prayer, this wonder and beauty that needed to be shared with his Father. Take some time to look at these astounding mountains. If you can do some hiking, perhaps plan for this opportunity. Allow these mountains to invite you to prayer. Share your experience of this place with your Father. Tell him about your experience of its beauty. Then, perhaps be silent. Imagine you and Jesus sitting side by side, letting the wonder of this place feed your soul and your prayer.

Prayer: Holy Jesus, be with me, sit with me and hear the prayer of my heart. Holy Spirit, invite me into the love that you share. Holy Father, allow me to be silent in your creation. Holy God, make me whole.

Allow these mountains to invite you to prayer.

Reading 27
Lamar Valley: Forgiveness and Renewal

Mark 1:4 *"And so John came, baptizing in the desert region and preaching a baptism of repentance for the forgiveness of sins." (NIV)*

BY THE MID-1920S, the grey wolf of Yellowstone no longer roamed the park, as they had been hunted into extinction within the area. However, started in the mid-1990s, a reintroduction program has seen wolves back in the park. The Lamar Valley is range to the Druid Pack, one of the most-sighted packs in the park. If you want to search for these beautiful creatures, this is the ideal spot.

Human communities, through greed or simple ignorance, have abused the natural world. We have hunted many creatures into extinction, we destroy habitat for unique species of plants and we have neglected to understand the complex workings of God's creation. However, God created nature to be forgiving. As the grey wolves were reintroduced to the park, so the ecological system that was needed to, once again, support them has begun to develop. Tree growth is changing, patterns of elk movement are changing, and there is increased food for beavers who are now breeding in the Northern part of the park again. All this is an amazing renewal of an ecosystem that existed before humans became involved.

This renewal is a glimpse of how abundantly God forgives us our greed and our ignorance. When asking for forgiveness, God pours his grace into us and we are transformed. There is new life, there is restoration, and new growth. Even if you do not see wolves, look at the valley. It is fundamentally different from what it was 10 years ago. This change was brought about because it was decided that we would protect, rather than destroy. One small change, one small and significant act of restoration, and the world begins to change. Imagine what God will be able to create if we are aware of our need to ask for forgiveness, for our need for restoration, and for our need for grace.

Prayer: "Amazing Grace, how sweet the sound, that saved a wretch like me. I once was lost, but now I'm found, was blind but now I see." Holy Jesus, help me to ask for forgiveness and accept renewal. Holy Spirit, pour your grace into my heart so that I am no longer blind.

(quote from Amazing Grace: John Newton)

One small change, one small and significant act of restoration, and the world begins to change.

Reading 28

Firehole River: Abundance

Jude 1:21 *"Keep yourselves in God's love as you wait for the mercy of our Lord Jesus Christ to bring you to eternal life."* (NIV)

THE FIREHOLE RIVER is one of the few places in the park where families are able to swim. It is more like a warm bath than a cooling swim, because water from a number of geysers drain into the river. The river is lined with aspens that dress in beautiful reds and golds in the autumn months. Levels of certain chemicals and minerals are at levels that should not support life, but trout still spawn in the river. Life in abundance is everywhere.

Life in abundance is what we are promised; however, we often define what we want this to mean. Often we define it in material terms. We want more money, more recognition, more and more and more. However, life in abundance has a different meaning for God. It is to create beauty and life in the hard, harsh places of this world. It is to support life where life may seem impossible. Abundance, as reflected in this place, is continual and constant creation. It is within this abundance that we are called to live. God defines what it is, and all we need to do is keep ourselves in God's love and to trust that something beautiful will come.

Prayer: Holy Creator, help me to rest in the abundance of your creation. Help me to wait within it for the mercy of your Son. Help me to trust your Spirit to lead me towards eternal life.

God defines what it is, and all we need to do is keep ourselves in God's love and to trust that something beautiful will come.

Reading 29
Lone Star Geyser: Wandering with God

Luke 24:15 "*As they talked and discussed these things with each other, Jesus himself came up and walked along with them*". *(NIV)*

THE LONE STAR Geyser is found at one of the back-trails of the Park. If you are visiting the Park in the peak season it provides a good opportunity to get out of the traffic and do an easy hike. Furthermore, there are no accurate postings on the times of eruption so you may have to take a book or a good fun group of friends to pass the time. Or, you could set this time aside for God.

Take a slow meditative walk along the trail. Take time to really look at the beauty around you. If you are walking with your kids, perhaps take some time to have those critical conversations that parents have with their children. Silently invite God into these conversations and trust that God will be there, gently listening. Enjoy simply being with God and resist the temptation to run ahead and get to your destination.

Spend some time walking with God in the light of God's love.

God does not seem to be interested in destinations, God seems to be interested in the path that is followed, the journeys that are taken and the relationships that are built. Thus, let yourself wander to Lone Star Geyser. If you miss the eruption, plan to sit and wait for the next. Step out of the hurley-burly of seeing every attraction, eruption, destination and meander with God for a while. You may be surprised at the journey you will take.

Prayer: Holy Jesus help me to take a step back, and gently wander with you along this trail. Help me not to rush or worry about what I will see or when I will see it. Holy Spirit fill my heart with peace so that I can focus on the journey rather than the destination.

Spend some time walking with God in the light of God's love.

Reading 30
Yellowstone National Park: Endings

Revelation 21:6 *"He said to me: "It is done. I am the Alpha and the Omega, the Beginning and the End. To him who is thirsty I will give to drink without cost from the spring of the water of life.' ." (NIV)*

ON LEAVING THE park, there is a bittersweet sense of ending. The magnificence and grandeur of mountains and geysers may have left you comfortably tired, and ready for a return to a more mundane life. The small hidden places of intense prayer are hopefully treasured in your heart. The many hours of happiness and reflection are captured on film to be remembered. Perhaps there is a desire to stay for a few more days, a desire that will return you to this park again and again. However, perhaps there is sadness, as you know that you will never visit again, or a realization that you are going home to a house empty of human companionship. Within this mix of emotions, remember that God is with you, at the beginning and at the end.

Remember that this park was created for the benefit and enjoyment of the people. Each person who makes the trip to the park is experiencing a place apart. In Christian tradition, places that are "set apart" are holy places. Places of encounter with God. Take these encounters, great or small, into the world. Remember too, that as this experience must end, others will begin. Take the treasures of this trip into those experiences. Finally, as you leave, know that God is with you in your going out and your coming in.

Prayer: As I take leave of this place, help me to treasure this time with you in my heart. Lead me ever deeper into your love and grace. God of creation, inspire me, God of redemption, forgive me, and God of love, enfold me. May I take the peace and challenge of Yellowstone into this world to the glory of your name.

Finally, as you leave, know that God is with you in your going out and your coming in.

About the Publisher

TheBiblePeople.com exists to encourage people to read, apply, and understand the Bible. Follow us at Facebook.com/TheBiblePeople

Other Titles by TheBiblePeople.com include:

30 Devotions for Women in Business

30 Devotions for Gardeners

Finding God in the Kitchen

Finding God in the Hunger Games

The Gospel According to Les Miserables

The Book of Proverbs Arranged by Topic

Every Prayer of the Bible

Made in the USA
Columbia, SC
18 May 2023

16958932R00063